WHO ELSE IN HISTORY?

Hidden Heroes in
SPACE
EXPLORATION

Dionna L. Mann

Lerner Publications ◆ Minneapolis

TO THE SCIENTISTS WHO HELP US DISCOVER THE AWESOME DESIGN WITHIN NATURE, FROM THAT INSIDE A CELL TO THAT AMID THE COSMOS

Lerner Publications Company
An imprint of Lerner Publishing Group, Inc.
241 First Avenue North
Minneapolis, MN 55401 USA

For reading levels and more information, look up this title at www.lernerbooks.com.

Main body text set in Aptifer Sans LT Pro.
Typeface provided by Linotype AG.

Lerner team: Sue Marquis

Library of Congress Cataloging-in-Publication Data

Names: Mann, Dionna L., author.
Title: Hidden heroes in space exploration / Dionna L. Mann.
Description: Minneapolis, MN : Lerner Publications, [2023] | Series: Alternator books. Who else in history? | Includes bibliographical references and index. | Audience: Ages 8–12 | Audience: Grades 4–6 | Summary: "Blast off to space with these hidden heroes. Discover astronauts, mathematicians, engineers, and more who defined space exploration"— Provided by publisher.
Identifiers: LCCN 2021045374 (print) | LCCN 2021045375 (ebook) | ISBN 9781728458427 (library binding) | ISBN 9781728464022 (paperback) | ISBN 9781728462561 (ebook)
Subjects: LCSH: Astronauts—United States—Biography—Juvenile literature. | African American astronauts—Biography—Juvenile literature. | Hispanic American astronauts—Biography—Juvenile literature. | Women astronauts—United States—Biography—Juvenile literature. | Astronautics personnel—United States—Biography—Juvenile literature. | African American mathematicians—Biography—Juvenile literature. | Minority engineers—United States—Biography—Juvenile literature. | LCGFT: Biographies.
Classification: LCC TL789.85.A1 M22 2023 (print) | LCC TL789.85.A1 (ebook) | DDC 629.450092/2—dc23

LC record available at https://lccn.loc.gov/2021045374
LC ebook record available at https://lccn.loc.gov/2021045375

Manufactured in the United States of America
1-50871-50208-1/13/2022

TABLE OF CONTENTS

BLAST OFF!

In 2020 three mission specialists were preparing to take the Starliner space module to the International Space Station (ISS). These specialists were Indian Slovenian American Sunita Williams, African American Jeanette Epps, and European American Josh Cassada.

Technicians prepare the Starliner for a test flight in 2021.

Williams completed four space walks from 2006 to 2007.

From the earliest days of the National Aeronautics and Space Administration (NASA), its scientists, like the Starliner crew, have come from all walks of life. Despite facing racism, sexism, and ableism, they've put their minds together to boldly explore space.

Epps earned a doctorate degree in aerospace engineering in 2000.

PAVING THE WAY

Before humans could land on the moon, many minds on the ground were needed to pave a way through Earth's atmosphere and back again.

An Apollo 11 module returns to the main space module in 1969. Dorothy Vaughan and Katherine Johnson helped make this mission possible.

DOROTHY VAUGHAN

Dorothy Vaughan, born in 1910 in Missouri, was a schoolteacher when she heard that the National Advisory Committee for Aeronautics (NACA) needed mathematicians. In 1943 she began working with the West Area Computers unit, a team of Black women mathematicians. They did complex calculations by hand and analyzed data about the forces of flight upon aircraft.

In 1949 Vaughan took charge of the unit, becoming NACA's first Black supervisor. Vaughan advocated for her team. "I changed what I could, and what I couldn't, I endured," she said.

NACA became NASA in 1958, and spaceflight became their top mission. Vaughan taught herself and her team FORTRAN, an early form of computer programming. It helped them make calculations to make spaceflight possible.

Vaughan worked on a program that sent the US's first satellites into space.

KATHERINE JOHNSON

Young Katherine, born in 1918 in West Virginia, counted anything and everything. She was one of the first Black students to enroll in the graduate program for mathematicians at West Virginia University. She could perform complex calculations by hand using simple tools like a slide rule and a protractor.

oughout her career, Johnson wrote or helped write twenty-six research papers.

In 1953 Johnson joined NACA's West Area Computers unit. Two weeks later, she was assigned to the Flight Research Division. She analyzed how airplanes were affected by sudden strong winds. She studied how they performed if caught inside powerful waves of wind that swirled behind moving aircraft.

When countries were competing to see who would be the first to go into space, Johnson joined NASA's Space Task Group. Her calculations for orbital spaceflights made America's first space journeys possible. She discovered how to send spacecraft into orbit and where Apollo 11 should land.

Johnson performs calculations on space navigation in 1962.

RACE YOU!

After the Soviet Union (a former nation that included Russia) launched a satellite called Sputnik, the United States raced to be the first to the moon.

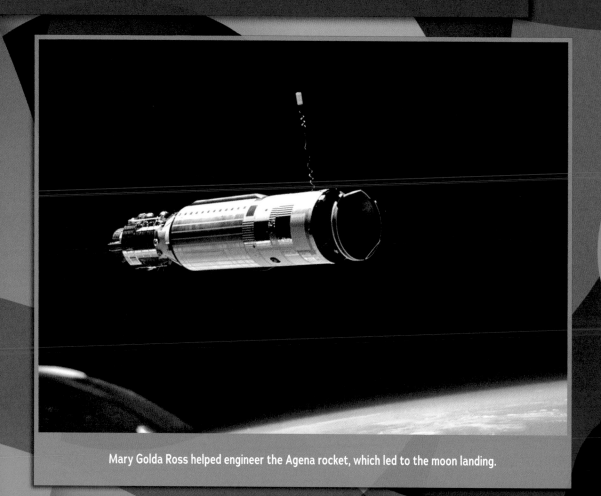

Mary Golda Ross helped engineer the Agena rocket, which led to the moon landing.

MARY GOLDA ROSS

Born in 1908 in Oklahoma, young Mary loved school. "I was brought up in the Cherokee tradition of equal education for boys and girls," she said. "It did not bother me to be the only girl in the math class, because math, chemistry and physics were more fun to study."

Ross became a rocket scientist and mathematician. She was the first Native American to earn an aerospace engineering degree.

Ross also studied how to make space travel to Mars and Venus a possibility.

CRITICAL THINKING

How would you feel if there was no one of your gender in your classes?

The Atlas-Agena rocket launches in 1967.

In 1942 Ross began working for Lockheed Missiles and Space Company. During the height of the space race, her team's research for NASA focused on the Atlas-Agena launch vehicle. Working day and night, they made sure the vehicle could handle the journey to the moon.

TAKE THIS WITH YOU!

Many NASA engineers have invented special equipment for astronauts to use in space to conduct science experiments.

George Carruthers (*center*) shows his Far Ultraviolet Electrographic Camera.

GEORGE CARRUTHERS

George Carruthers was born in 1939 in Ohio. When he was ten, he built a telescope with cardboard and a lens. Reading science fiction books got him interested in space.

In 1964 he earned a PhD in aeronautical and astronautical engineering. As a research scientist, he invented the Far Ultraviolet Electrographic Camera. NASA attached his invention to a rocket that flew above Earth's atmosphere. His camera proved that molecular hydrogen, a type of gas, exists in space. This helped scientists understand how stars form.

ruthers holds a film case from a telescope he designed.

The Far Ultraviolet Electrographic Camera is placed on the moon and takes photos in 1972.

In 1972 the Apollo 16 crew placed Carruthers's camera on the moon. They pointed it at Earth to learn more about its atmosphere. They pointed it at other faraway objects like giant clouds of stellar dust and gas. In all, they took 178 pictures.

ABOARD THE SHUTTLES

These astronauts boarded shuttles to blast off into space. They performed experiments, worked on new technology, and fulfilled their dreams.

Astronaut Mae C. Jemison completes part of an experiment in 1992.

Guion (Guy) Bluford Jr.

Guion (Guy) Bluford Jr. was born in 1942 in Pennsylvania. Growing up, Guy wanted to be an engineer like his dad. He became an aerospace engineer. After being an air force fighter pilot, Bluford began training as a NASA astronaut in 1978. He was a mission specialist on four space shuttle flights.

His first flight was aboard the STS-8 mission that launched in 1983. Bluford became the first Black American in space. While orbiting Earth at 180,000 miles (289,682 km) per hour, Bluford said, "You don't see borders. So you recognize that this is a very small planet . . . and we all have to take care of it together."

...ord joined the US Astronaut Hall of Fame in 2010.

FRANKLIN CHANG-DÍAZ

Franklin Chang-Díaz was born in 1950 in Costa Rica. When Franklin was a kid, he and his cousins would lie on their backs inside a cardboard box, pretending they were astronauts.

After immigrating to the United States, Chang-Díaz earned degrees in mechanical engineering and physics. In 1981 he became a NASA astronaut. When the shuttle Columbia took off on January 12, 1986, he was the first Latin American to fly in space. During liftoff, he remembered how, as children, he and his cousins pretended to be astronauts. He said, "I felt I had already done this before."

g-Díaz spent more than sixty-six days in space.

Chang-Díaz flew on seven shuttle flights and did three space walks. In 1993 he became the director of the Johnson Space Center's Advanced Space Propulsion Laboratory. In 2021 his company was researching a new type of engine for faster space travel.

Chang-Díaz also studied rocket propulsion and came up with a special engine to improve space travel.

CRITICAL THINKING

Why is representation important? How would you feel if there weren't any scientists who looked like you? How would a lack of representation impact science?

SALLY RIDE

Sally Ride, born in 1951 in California, was a graduate physics student when she heard NASA wanted women astronauts. She applied for their astronaut program and was accepted!

In 1983 Ride boarded the STS-7 flight on the Challenger and became the first American woman in space. She worked a robotic arm that was used to deploy a satellite.

After her time at NASA, Ride founded Sally Ride Science, a program that encourages students, especially girls, to pursue STEM careers. She also started EarthKAM and MoonKAM, which allowed middle schoolers to request specific pictures of Earth and the moon taken from cameras on the ISS and on two lunar orbiters.

...er second space mission, Ride studied Earth.

"The thing that I'll remember m
about the flight is that it was fun
fact, I'm sure it was the most fun
ever have in my life."

—SALLY RIDE

d fellow astronauts blast off
ard the Challenger in 1983

MAE C. JEMISON

Mae C. Jemison was born in 1956. When she was young, Mae stared at the stars and imagined visiting them. Seeing Nichelle Nichols play Lieutenant Uhura on *Star Trek* fueled her imagination. She also kept up with the Apollo program. Jemison became an astronaut in 1987.

Aboard the shuttle Endeavour in 1992, Jemison became the first Black American woman in space. As a medical doctor, she took the lead in several experiments in the shuttle's Spacelab-J. One experiment investigated the effect of spaceflight on bone cells.

Looking down on Chicago, where she grew up, Jemison wondered how her younger self would feel about her flight. "I think she would've been tickled," she said.

After working at NASA, Jemison led 100 Year Starship, a project aimed to make human space travel to another star a reality in the next hundred years.

wants to make sure science and technology are accessible to all people.

JOHN HERRINGTON

In 1958 in Oklahoma, John Herrington was born into the Chickasaw Nation. When he was a kid, John loved soaring in his dad's airplane, but he dreamed of flying higher.

Herrington joined the US Navy and became a pilot. He earned degrees in mathematics and aeronautical engineering. In 1996 he became an astronaut. In 2002 he boarded the Endeavour space shuttle STS-113. He became the first enrolled Native American to walk in space when his crew did installation work on the ISS.

Herrington took with him to space sweetgrass, eagle feathers, arrowheads, a wooden flute, and a flag of the Chickasaw Nation to represent his heritage.

As part of the Astronaut Support Personnel team, Herrington prepared for launches and completed tas after landings.

"Flying in space is an incredible experience. It's just a remarkable adventure. It's been a real privilege to do that."

—JOHN HERRINGTON

The Endeavour takes off in 2002 with Herrington and other astronauts aboard.

Ellen Ochoa

Ellen Ochoa, born in 1958 in California, was in graduate school when she saw Sally Ride fly into space. Ride's journey helped Ochoa realize it was possible for her.

Ochoa applied for NASA's astronaut program, but she wasn't accepted. However, being a physicist and an electrical engineer, she got a research job with NASA. While there, she was a coinventor on three patents for an optical inspection system that makes photos from space clearer.

The second time Ochoa applied to be an astronaut, she was accepted! In 1993, aboard the space shuttle Discovery, she became the first Latina in space. Ochoa went on four space missions. One made the first shuttle docking with the ISS.

On the ISS, Ochoa looks out a window at Earth in 2002.

MISSION CONTROL CENTER

Whenever NASA launches a flight, there is a ground crew in a control room. They pay attention to computer screens to make sure everything goes as planned.

Johanna Lucht plays an essential role in NASA's launches.

JOHANNA LUCHT

Johanna Lucht, who is deaf, was born in Germany in 1992 to hearing parents. At first, no one around her knew American Sign

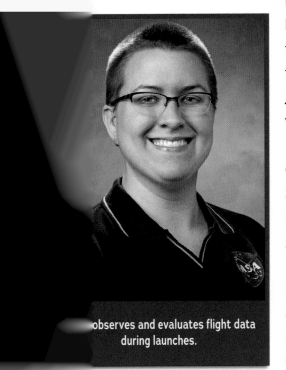

...observes and evaluates flight data during launches.

Language (ASL). She was nine when her school finally provided someone to teach her ASL. Then she was able to read and write and communicate. Johanna's family moved to the US when she was twelve.

While earning a computer science degree, Lucht interned at NASA. She developed a collision-avoidance mobile app for pilots. After she graduated, NASA offered her a job.

On April 4, 2017, Lucht became NASA's first Deaf engineer to have an active role in a control room. She monitored the inflight data of the Gulfstream III, a research aircraft. The crew was testing twisted wing flaps. Lucht's interpreter, using video streaming, signed all inflight communications to her.

TO THE STARS

There are numerous hidden heroes of space in the historical record. They created new technology, helped send people to space, and traveled there. These heroes all have one thing in common: they kept looking up toward the stars.

TIMELINE

1942: Mary Golda Ross begins working for Lockheed Missiles and Space Company.

1949: Dorothy Vaughan takes the lead of the West Area Computers unit, becoming NACA's first Black supervisor.

1953: Katherine Johnson begins working for NACA's West Area Computers unit.

1972: George Carruthers's camera is placed on the lunar surface by the Apollo 16 astronauts.

1983: Sally Ride becomes the first American woman to fly into space.

Guion (Guy) Bluford Jr. becomes the first Black American to fly into space.

1986: Franklin Chang-Díaz becomes the first Hispanic American to fly into space.

1992: Mae C. Jemison becomes the first Black American woman to fly into space.

1993: Ellen Ochoa becomes the first Latina to fly into space.

2002: John Herrington becomes the first enrolled Native American to fly into space.

2017: Johanna Lucht becomes NASA's first Deaf American in a control center during a crewed test flight.

Glossary

ableism: discrimination or prejudice against individuals with disabilities

aeronautics: the study, design, and making of machines related to air flight

mathematician: someone who specializes in math

orbit: the path an object in space takes when it goes around another object in space, like Earth's path around our sun

physics: the study of matter and its motion and how matter interacts with and reacts to other matter, energy, and other forces

satellite: an artificial body placed in orbit around Earth or the moon or another planet to collect information or for communication

stellar: relating to a star or stars

Source Notes

7 Lorna Hutchman, "Dorothy Vaughan: NASA's Overlooked Star," Science Museum, September 20, 2020, https://blog .sciencemuseum.org.uk/nasas-overlooked-star/.

11 "People of Color in STEM: Mary Golda Ross," Colorado State University, April 27, 2021, https://cowyamp.colostate.edu/people -of-color-in-stem-mary-golda-ross/.

17 "Guy Bluford: Reaching for the Stars—Conversations from Penn State," YouTube video, 26:30, posted by WPSU, December 19, 2013, https://www.youtube.com/watch?v=wr9s377Lpn0.

18 "Profile of Franklin Chang-Díaz," YouTube video, 2:24, posted by NASA, May 19, 2013, https://www.youtube.com/watch?v=o _Rnz2Pl5Bc.

21 "Dr. Sally Ride," Sally Ride Science at UC San Diego, accessed August 8, 2021, https://sallyridescience.ucsd.edu/about /sallyride/about-sallyride/.

22 "Mae Jemison: I Wanted to Go into Space," PBS, July 31, 2014, https://www.pbs.org/video/secret-life-scientists-mae-jemison-i-wanted-go-space/.

24 "John Herrington: I Dreamed of Being an Astronaut," Chickasaw TV Video Network, 1:02, accessed August 8, 2021, https://www.chickasaw.tv/playlists/renaissance-videos/videos/john-herrington-profiles-of-a-nation-part-2.

Learn More

Alexander, Heather. *Dr. Mae Jemison: Brave Rocketeer*. New York: Harper, 2021.

Biography: George Carruthers
https://www.biography.com/inventor/george-carruthers

Kim, Carol. *Hidden Heroes in Technology*. Minneapolis: Lerner Publications, 2023.

NASA: Dr. Ellen Ochoa
https://www.nasa.gov/centers/johnson/about/people/orgs/bios/ochoa.html

NASA Space Place: Science and Technology
https://spaceplace.nasa.gov/menu/science-and-technology/

Rector, Rebecca Kraft. *International Space Station*. New York: Children's Press, 2022.

Science Buddies: 21 Scientists and Engineers to Learn More About
https://www.sciencebuddies.org/blog/hispanic-scientists-engineers

Sorell, Traci. *Classified: The Secret Career of Mary Golda Ross, Cherokee Aerospace Engineer*. Minneapolis: Milbrook Press, 2021.

Index

Photo Acknowledgments

Image credits: NASA, pp. 4, 5 (Epps), 6, 8, 9, 10, 13, 14, 15, 16, 17, 18, 19, 20, 21, 22, 23, 24, 25, 28, 29; NASA/Robert Markowitz/Wikimedia Commons, p. 5 (Williams); NASA on The Commons/flickr, p. 7; Pictures From History/Newscom, pp. 11, 28 (Ross); NASA/Wikimedia Commons, p. 12; NASA/Lauren Hughes, p. 26; NASA/Ken Ulbrich, p. 27.

Cover: NASA.